What's My Style?

Test and Study Secrets for Procrastinating Teens

An Owner's Manual for Your Brain

D1111540

Betty Caldwell M.A.

Outskirts Press, Inc.
Denver, Colorado

Outskirts Press, Inc.
http://www.outskirtspress.com

ISBN: 978-1-4327-3476-3

Outskirts Press and the "OP" logo are trademarks belonging to Outskirts Press, Inc.

PRINTED IN THE UNITED STATES OF AMERICA

Table of Contents

Acknowledgments

Thank you to my intellectual inspirations, Temple Grandin, who first captured my attention with her book on thinking in pictures, Linda Kreger Silverman, PhD, who led the way with her groundbreaking work on visual-spatial learners, and Jeffrey Freed and Laurie Parsons who understood the continuum of brain-based learning. Deep appreciation to Jill Bolte Taylor, PhD, for making available to the world her personal journey into the workings of the right and left brain. To John J. Ratey, M. D., and Richard Restak, M.D. for their writings on how the brain works.

To Buck Jones, (www.buckjonesillustrator.com) nationally known humorous illustrator, for his warm and wonderful illustrations for this book, and a true partner in this work.

Most especially, I am grateful to all of my students, their parents, and the educators and administrators in the Howard County School System who have been an essential part of the development of The Stressless Tests® Method. Special thanks to all my students who offered their advice on how to write a book on studying that they might actually read!

Finally, I send my thanks to Jason Shulman who taught me how teach to each and every student in the class. And finally, deep appreciation to Brenda Blessings, who cheered me on from the beginning.

How and Why You Should Read This Book: This is An Owner's Manual for Your Brain

At last, I am learning who I am, instead of who I'm not.

–High School Student

Don't tell people how to live their lives. Tell them stories, and

they will figure it out.

–Randy Pausch, The Last Lecture

Are you a master of procrastination? I mean, really excellent

at putting things off?

Are you someone who:

doesn't test well, despite doing well in class?

is easily distracted and frequently bored?

is great with complex issues but stymied by simple ones?

sometimes loses track of time, finding hours have gone by?

has a movie rolling in your head most of the time?

has trouble focusing in class?

loves the big picture but is frustrated by the details?

is more random than systematic?

If any or all of these are true...great! Welcome. This is the book for you. Think of it as an owner's manual for your brain. It is time someone made sense of all these traits for you, so you will know more about yourself, your gifts, and your quirks. And, to teach you how to access even more parts of your brain to make learning simpler and more rewarding.

Fully 50% of Americans think just like you do. The problem is, as you probably know, this type of thinking is not rewarded when it comes to test-based results in school. Most of you have not been taught how to use your learning style to your advantage. In this book, you will find out more about how you learn as an individual, and best of all, how to recognize and access the part of your intelligence you need in a given situation.

You can be your random and creative self, or when you choose, you can tap a different part of you brain and do very well on tests.

As it turns out, if you recognize yourself from the above description, your brain has decided for you that you process information in a random way, are a people person, think creatively, and usually know what works for you and what doesn't. In terms of learning, your style may be called right-brain learning, visual-spatial, or intuitive. In this book, I will use the terms right-brain and left-brain learners. You will quickly recognize yourself, your parents, friends, and teachers and you will reach a whole new level of understanding of the importance of learning style. I invite you to read on.

What's My Style is based on Nobel-prize winning research and the latest findings in brain science. It captures the essence of my Stressless Tests® Method of self-understanding and study tips, which I have taught to thousands of students over the past five years. Here you will learn of the great gifts and advantages of your way of processing information. You will also learn how to use your unique skills to your advantage and how to study slightly differently to become a master of testing. This is groundbreaking work, and you will enjoy seeing the results in your own life.

Try to read Chapter One first. If you fill out the questionnaire in order to determine your learning style, then the rest of the book will make a lot more sense. You may read the remaining chapters in any order you choose. Use it as a mirror to see yourself more clearly. Do you recognize the descriptions? Are the stories familiar to you? Notice the tips that can help you to use your unique talents, and to access parts of your learning capacity that have been hidden until now. Enjoy the stories. Enjoy your self-discovery.

WELCOME PARENTS

Chances are, you have been puzzled and confused by your child when it comes to his or her schoolwork. How is it, for example, that she could be doing advanced level work, excelling in class work, and yet doing poorly on tests? Why don't your suggestions help him get organized? And how is it even possible for him to get the answers right on his math test when he can't show his work? In sum, how is it that such an obviously bright, all-around great kid can think so differently from you? Read on.

To start with, read Chapter One. Fill out the Left-Brain Right-Brain Continuum Questionnaire for yourself. Find out whether you prefer to process information primarily through the right or left hemisphere of your brain. Ask your son or daughter how they scored. If you have found yourself knocking heads over studying, chances are there are some fundamental differences at work.

Next, enjoy the stories. See if you recognize some of the habits you see in your student, and realize that they are a reflection of their brain-based style. Finally, to learn more about how to effectively support your student, look at the skill-based materials. Above all, I invite you to read on with a spirit of openness and curiosity, never judgment.

WHAT'S MY STYLE?

Your Learning Style: What Difference Does It Make?

Imagine what would happen if, as a child, you had saved pennies. No other coins, just pennies. You stashed them away in a piggy bank until it was chock full. Then, after some time, you headed out for a vending machine to get a nice cold drink. You looked forward to having a treat as a reward for all the time you spent saving your pennies.

We know, of course, that it wouldn't be a happy outcome. Vending machines are picky. They may take dimes, nickels, quarters, or dollar bills, but they won't take pennies. All your efforts will have been in vain. Your hopes for a treat will be dashed, and chances are you will be pretty frustrated. In your head, you will hear some version of, "But I have the money!"

This is a pretty good illustration of why it is you can study for a test, know the material thoroughly, and still not do well—

because you have stored the material in such a way that you can't use it. You have stored it in the wrong part of your brain.

Your brain has a definite opinion on how it prefers to learn. It is rooted in your biology and is the result of something that occurred before you were four. Then, for a reason no one as yet understands, one side of your brain became the dominant side. And although each side, or hemisphere, of the brain looks the same, they have dramatically different ways of learning. Think of each side as having its own personality.

Are you good at procrastinating, or are you always on time? Do you pay attention to details, or are you a big picture thinker? These are just a few of the differences you will notice, depending on whether the left side or right side of your brain is in charge. Is it easy for you to stay focused, or do you get bored and drift off? You may be surprised to learn how much of your life is affected by your built-in learning style.

The best way to understand your learning style is to think in terms of a continuum. (Think of a timeline. A continuum is a sequence of indicators, in which the extremes are quite different from each other. Think of height. Everyone has height: some are tall, and some are short.) So it is with our learning style. It is not about being exclusively a left-brain or a right-brain thinker. We all have and use both sides. It is a question of how strong the brain's preference is for one side or the other. I think of it in terms of which side of the brain speaks up first, and how long it takes for the other side to chime in! Understanding where you are on the continuum will open up a lot of insight for you into how you learn, where your challenges are, and why you have many of your personal habits.

What's My Style?

Try the following activities to determine your style. They are quick and easy. After you take these steps, you will know a lot more about your brain preference and what difference it makes in your life and learning.

Step One: The Hot Fudge Sundae Test

First, stop and think about a hot fudge sundae.

Now, quickly examine your response. Did you see a picture of the hot fudge sundae in your mind's eye? If so, that tells you that your brain automatically converted words into pictures. You didn't have to try to see it. It just happened. That is a good indicator that you are a right-brain thinker. (Some of my students report they not only see it, they also taste it.) For right-brain thinkers, it is as though pictures are your first language. You literally think in pictures.

If you didn't see a picture of it, you may be a left-brain thinker. You didn't see a picture of it; you just know what it is.

Step Two: Yes or No?

Next, take a moment to fill in the *Left-Brain Right-Brain Continuum Questionnaire.* Don't over think it. Simply answer yes or no to each question.

If it could be either answer, think about which is true more often, even if it is just fifty-one percent of the time. When you have completed all the questions, count and record the number of yes answers.

Scoring

According to Jeffrey Freed and Laurie Parsons who developed this questionnaire, the higher your score, the stronger you are in your right-brain thinking. If you scored 0–4, you are very left-brained, 5–8, somewhat left-brained, 9–12, whole brained, 13–16, somewhat right-brained, and 17–20, very right-brained.

In my experience, anyone who scores 9–10 is likely to lead with a right-brain response, but quickly also voice a left-brain thought. As one student said, "When it comes to homework, my right brain says 'Do it later,' but my left brain then says, 'Get it over with!'" Those who score 12 or above are more likely to give a right-brain response most of the time. These are the students who are more likely to participate actively in classroom discussions, frequently guessing at answers rather than thinking it through. Their answers are creative, and frequently both fun and funny. They often give feeling-based responses, such as "I hate math!" or "My Mom is going to kill me if I fail this test!"

LEFT-BRAIN RIGHT-BRAIN CONTINUUM QUESTIONNAIRE

Quickly read and answer yes or no to each question below. If it seems like the answer is sometimes yes and sometimes no, choose the one which is true more often, even it is just slightly more than half the time. For some questions, such as the ones about handwriting and slow development, you may know the answer only if someone else has told you. (Do people tell you they can't read your writing? Do your parents say you were slow to walk? If not, assume the answer is No.)

	NO	YES
1. Are you better at remembering faces than names?	_____	_____
2. When presented with something to put together, such as a toy or piece of furniture, are you likely to discard the printed directions and figure out for yourself how to build it?	_____	_____
3. Are you better at thinking of ideas if you are left alone to concentrate, rather than working with a group?	_____	_____
4. Do you rely mostly on pictures to remember things, as opposed to names and words?	_____	_____
5. Do you have especially acute (good) hearing?	_____	_____

	NO	YES

6. Do you cut the labels out of your clothes? Do you favor clothes that are especially soft and well worn, finding most clothes too rough or scratchy?

7. Do you tend to put yourself down a lot?

8. When you are asked to spell a word, do you "see" it in your head, rather than sound it out phonetically?

9. When studying a subject, do you prefer to get the "big picture" as opposed to learning a lot of facts?

10. Are you good with puzzles and mazes?

11. Can you imagine things in three dimensions? Can you imagine a cube in your head, rotate it and easily view it from every angle?

12. Do you need to like your teacher to do well in a class?

13. Are you easily distracted to the point you find yourself daydreaming a lot?

14. Are you a perfectionist to the point it gets in the way of trying new things?

15. Are you ultra-competitive, hating to lose more than most people do?

16. Are you good at figuring people out? Do others tell you that you are good at "reading" people?

	NO	YES
17. Is your handwriting below average or poor?	____	____
18. When you are in a new place, do you find your way around easily?	____	____
19. Were you considered a late bloomer?	____	____
20. Were you a late walker, or did you have other delayed motor skills as a child?	____	____

When you have completed the questions, count and record the number of YES answers. [1]

Total number of YES answers   _____

MY SCORE IS _____

I AM A _____ -BRAIN THINKER

---

[1] Reprinted with the permission of Simon & Schuster, Inc. from RIGHT-BRAINED CHILDREN IN A LEFT-BRAINED WORLD: Unlocking the Potential of Your ADD Child by Jeffrey Freed & Laurie Parsons. Copyright © 1997 by Jeffrey Freed and Laurie Parsons. All rights reserved. [1]

KNOCKING HEADS
WITH PARENTS

In the last class of one of my high school courses, one of the students asked, "Do you ever teach this to parents?" His friend, who had joked his way through much of the course, spoke up with surprising intensity. *"I would pay you to teach this to my parents. They have totally unrealistic expectations for me."* Both boys are strong right-brain learners. Their parents? I would have to guess that they lead with their left brain. What's the problem?

Remember, it is as though each side of the brain has its own personality, and its own view of how to get things done. When students and their parents have strongly differing learning styles, and no understanding of what that means, it can lead to conflict, frustration, family stress, and a sense of disempowerment.

Parents, on the other hand, call and ask, "Why can't my child get organized?" (I have learned that, before they call, many parents have invested a lot of time in trying to teach their child the "right way" to get organized. Color-coding. Notes in their locker. Complex file systems. None of which worked.) These are, of course, great strategies for an analytical, detail-oriented, left-brain learner. But they may make no sense at all to a right-brain student.

Other popular questions include, "Why does she procrastinate so much?" "How is it even possible that he is bright and does well in class, but not on tests?"

It is important to remember that part of the left-brain perspective is that there is a "right way" to do things. It can sound like this:

"You should always do your homework as soon as you get home from school."

"You need to study at least an hour for every test."

"You don't get a break until you have finished all your studies."

The right brain is more attuned to what actually works for it. The basis for that understanding is not a rigid formula, but *what actually works!* Self-monitoring is a large part of a right-brain student's discovery of what works for them. It is more of an inner knowing, rather than an exterior rule. A favorite right-brain saying is, "It depends!" *This is a huge difference in perspective!*

Right-brain students may realize that they need to do something physically active, or simply chill out after school before they are ready to hit the books again. Or, with a photographic memory, they may be able to prepare for a test in a much shorter time than one would expect.

One friend told me a story from her high school days. Her assignment was to memorize the Periodic Table of the Elements. She'd had several weeks to complete the task, but had procrastinated in getting started, despite her mother's pleas. Finally, the night before the due date, her mother, thoroughly frustrated, looked her in the eye and said, "You know you are going to fail!" Stung, the student retreated to her room, spent an hour absorbing the table into her visual memory, then emerged and triumphantly reported, "I'm done!"

What is the solution to this dilemma? Parents and students can start by determining what their learning style is. Follow the instructions in Chapter One to find out. Share your scores. Keep reading the following chapters to learn more about each other's outlook. Be curious about how each one sees the world. You may well be intrigued and decide to experiment with some new ways of doing things to see if they work for you.

As one father noted, "I'm going to spend a lot less time helping my daughter with her homework, now that I know how she actually learns." He went on to recount his frustration as he explained over and over again the formula used to explain air density.

Finally, he went to the freezer and took out a bag of frozen peas, pointing out the difference in density between the peas and the air in between them. Now, with a concrete visual example she could understand, his daughter responded, "Well, why didn't you say so in the first place?"

A foolish consistency is the hobgoblin of little minds...

Ralph Waldo Emerson

What's Wrong with Doing It Right?

You know I'm not like anyone else, cause One Size never fits.

–Singer/Songwriter Matt Andersen

6 foot 2 and 400 pounds

As my students experiment with what they are learning about their own study style, they begin to report successes. "I got a B on my biology test, and it wasn't even hard!" is a typical comment. They practice getting clear in their intent, focusing, taking study breaks, and putting everything into words. It works like a charm. And then, in almost every class, after about the third week, I hear this: "I finished studying, and knew I was ready for the exam. Then, my dad said, 'Go back and study for another hour. You should spend two hours on your homework every night.'" Uh-oh, the dreaded "Right Way" strikes again. Now what?

Remember, the "right way to do things" idea is a left-brain construct. It is said as though there is one, and only one, way to do things right. As though any other way is wrong. Note that it is said as though the rule is always true for everyone, no matter what. The problem is, we know that people process information differently, and can arrive at learning by very different paths. You may demonstrate remarkable creativity along the way.

How do you know how much studying is enough? It is important to know. For right-brain learners, self-testing is the key. Can you talk about the material in your own words? Are you confident you know the answers? Have you followed the study habits that work best for you?

- Remember, set your target in advance for what you want to accomplish. (For example, say it is to memorize the entire list of vocabulary words and their definitions.)

- Test yourself. See if you can do it. Can you speak the list out loud, using your own words? Are you listening to yourself? Do you know you know it?

- *For right-brain thinkers, it is all about observable results based on self-observation, not just "doing it right."*

- Don't ignore the rules. Just be curious to see if they actually help you, or if you have a better way. Do what works for you.

INTENT

The Hidden Dimension is Your Intent

The single most important step for you in moving up to the next level is to learn about your intent. It is the key to doing your personal best in everything you do—on the field, on stage, in class, or anywhere.

Your intent is simply defined as what you really want to do. Not what your parents, your teachers, or your friends want you to do, but what *you* want to do. It's an inner impulse, and it is incredibly powerful. It has a huge impact on what you do and how well you succeed.

One powerful example of intent in action is the story of Jordan Snipes, a college basketball player. With just 0.6 (six-tenths) of a second left in overtime, Jordan, who played for Guilford College, rebounded the other team's missed free throw, wheeled around, and heaved the ball the full length of the court.

With his team down by 2, and with just six-tenths of a second left, it is astonishing that Jordan was still totally engaged in the game—still intent on winning it. Even the coaches thought the game was over, and were walking toward each other on the sidelines to shake hands. Then they noticed a ball sailing by from the end of the court. They stopped in their tracks and watched it go in, producing an unexpected win.

On the court, Jordan was so engaged in winning the game that he was planning his strategy, moment by moment. At first, he was planning to grab the rebound and lean against one of the opposing players, drawing a foul. Then the opposing coach told his players to back away from the line.

Jordan reported, "When they did that, I couldn't get near anybody in six-tenths of a second, so I just took the ball and threw it. I didn't know what else to do."

To see Jordan's play, go to youtube.com and enter "the world's most amazing basketball shot."

As you can see, it all started with Jordan's intent to win the game. Improbably, with just six-tenths of a second on the clock, he realized that he wanted to win and was willing to do something to make it happen. So, he did the only thing that came to mind.

I promise you this. Being clear and focused in your intent will always make a difference. It is the difference between being awake, alert, and focused on what you want to accomplish, and being mentally asleep, unfocused, and unaware of why you are doing what you are doing. Things will happen that will amaze you.

THE MAGIC STEP: SETTING YOUR INTENT

There are several easy steps in setting your intent.

First, get in touch with what you really want to do. Be clear. Do you want to get an A on your math test? Finish your homework in time to get to soccer practice? Stay calm and focused as you give an in-class presentation? Once you are clear, write it down.

Next, add in any other specifics that occur to you to flesh it out. Perhaps you want to stay calm and focused on your in-class presentation, and meet the assigned time frame of 10 minutes. Do you also want to enjoy giving it? It is good to be specific about what you want, and be as detailed as possible.

Finally, state the outcome you want for doing this. What is the benefit to you? For example, your statement might be, "I want to be calm and focused during my presentation, completing it in 10 minutes, and feeling personally connected to my classmates so that I will build my confidence in giving presentations. I want to get a positive review from my class and teacher."

Once you have created this statement, you will naturally think of the action steps you need to take. Ask yourself, "What do I need to fulfill my intent?" Jot down whatever occurs to you.

You may hear that you need to practice it out loud, or set the timer to clock how long it takes. Perhaps you would like a friend or your family to be your practice audience. Or, do you need to have the presentation written in an extra-large font, so you can easily refer to it as you stand in front of the class? Think of the kinds of presentations that have gotten good reviews, so you know the framework in which you are working.

This is where your natural creativity will help you. Remember, your question is, "What do I need," not "What is the right way to do this?" Your creativity is a great companion; use it! Finally, enjoy the outcome and notice how much difference it makes when you are clear in your intent.

When you are aware of your intentions, you are no longer surprised by the consequences they create.

Gary Zukav

Your Intent in Action

Take a moment to think about something you love doing. It might be playing a sport, performing, reading, or anything you do because you enjoy it. Now, in your mind's eye, see yourself engaged in that activity. Enjoy the movie unwinding in your head. Imagine the details clearly and feel the feelings and sensations involved. Let it come to life in as many of your senses as possible.

Now, can you stop action and say what your intent was in that moment? How clear were you? Did it make a difference?

In one class, Ryan said he imagined he was playing football on his high school team. He had just caught the ball and was running for a touchdown. Of course, his intent was clear! Can you imagine him saying, "Hmm, should I catch the ball? Or just watch it sail by? Catch it and then just stop running?" No, he was clear, focused, and energized.

Lauren said she saw herself competing in a horse show, getting ready to go over a jump. She vividly described the subtle movements with her hands, her knees, and shifting weight to prepare herself and her horse for the jump. One momentary lapse on her part could spook her horse, or knock her off balance. She knew exactly what to do, and she was totally into it. That is having a clear intent.

Practice becoming aware of your intent in every situation. Having a clear, positive, and focused intent will always make a difference.

TEST TAKING

...through our understanding that we have two very distinct ways of being in the world, we can deliberately choose to have much more power over what's going on inside our brains than we ever imagined!
Jill Bolte Taylor, Ph.D

Thinking Like a Test

"I know I know it. How come I don't test well?"

Think about the characteristics of a typical test. Most tests

- use words, not pictures

- ask for information, not feelings

- have right and wrong answers

- are graded objectively, not by how much someone

  likes you

- involve details, and

- have a time limit.

Based on this list, which side of your brain needs to be in charge in order for you to take a test successfully? The left brain, of course. The one that thinks in words, knows right and wrong, thinks in time, is detail oriented, etc.

But, if you are primarily a right-brain learner, you master information in a totally different way, which does not show up well on tests. You can know a subject thoroughly, and still not test well. How is this possible?

Consider this question: Do you know how to get from your school to your home? Meaning, if someone offered you a ride home from school, could you sit in the front seat of the car and tell them when to turn left and when to turn right to get to your house? Of course you could. In fact, if you heard you were going to have a test on how to get to your house from school, you would be very confident, because you would *know* you know!

But then, suppose you had to write down, starting from the school's parking lot, every turn, whether right or left, and the exact name of every street. And then you had to list every stop sign or stoplight, every landmark (like a gas station or a big building), and finally, you had to list the *exact* mileage. Suddenly, what seemed like a snap becomes almost impossible. What you know in your visual right brain, you must describe from your left brain.

Why is it so hard? Think of it as though you haven't stored it in your left brain in the first place. How can you retrieve something from a place in which you haven't stored it? (Imagine trying to take money out of a bank account to which you have made no deposits.)

This explains the disappointing experience of feeling very confident before a test (you know you know!), and then getting a poor grade. It is always a shock and never fun. It can be demoralizing. And, how can you explain it to your parents?

The Simple Secret

If you are a right-brain learner, you may need to change the way you study for tests. It's not hard, and you can do it. In fact, you will be surprised at what a huge difference a little change will make. It is all about using words.

Remember, as a right-brain learner, you are thinking in pictures, storing information in a series of still pictures or short movies in your head. For a test, or to make an oral report, you need to be able to convert the pictures to words. Start today to use words actively as you study. When preparing for a test, review the material by saying the answers out loud. Use your own words to explain new concepts. Don't forget to actually pay attention to yourself as you speak! (You know what I mean. You have heard people read whole passages out loud without being able to say what they just read.)

When you are using words, you are getting your left brain involved. Study by yourself, or with friends, or have your parents quiz you. Why? Not to show them you know the material but to force you to use words.

Here is another tip. It is about what to do with those pictures that show up in your head as you study. Use them! Simply use your words to describe the images. It will give you a great boost as you tap into what you know.

A True Story

I once coached a doctor who was preparing for a major professional exam, the medical boards. Her career depended on her passing the test. She had failed it twice, and had one last time to pass it. Of course, she was stressed to the max.

In one of our sessions, I asked her a sample question about a particular kind of surgery. She froze. Then she struggled to find a way to describe all the steps involved, but couldn't. We stopped, and I helped her relax out of the stress. Next, I asked her the same question again. To my astonishment, she began to describe the surgery in total, vivid detail, going on and on with great confidence until I stopped her. "What happened?" I asked. With a huge smile, she said, "I've done that surgery. I could see the movie of it in my head. So, I just described the movie!"

Diary or Text Message?

Focus for a minute on your preparation for tests. If you are a right-brain thinker, your study style may guarantee that what you learn is available only to you. It is as though, without meaning to, you file the information away in a locked diary. You know what's in there, but nobody else can see it. The result is that you will know the material, but your teacher won't know that you know.

You want your test response to be more like a text message. You want to send information that is clear, easy to read, and understandable. You want your message to be successfully received. It is for this reason that you need to study by speaking out loud. Make sure you involve your language center. After all, that's its job—to communicate with others.

Test Anxiety Tips

Nobody likes to take a test. Some level of nervousness in preparing for and taking a test is normal. It can serve as a motivator and provide some extra adrenalin to help you do your best. But too much nervousness can be a problem. If you know the material and have studied well, but find you freeze up during the test, you are experiencing test anxiety.

Tip Number One: Do Relaxation Breathing

This is your number one tool. You will be amazed at how effective this practice is. It will help you to calm down and focus. Take a minute to try it out now. It's easy.

When to use this practice:

> before or during a test
>
> when you are frustrated
>
> when you need to calm down and focus in class
>
> before speaking to the class

before and during any athletic game,

cheerleading, performance, etc.

before falling asleep

any time!

Steps to take:

1. Sit comfortably with both feet flat on the floor. Let your back be relaxed but straight.

2. Close your eyes or look at a spot on the floor right in front of you.

3. Breathe naturally, and notice where you feel the air when you breathe in. You may feel it on your nose or your upper lip.

4. When you breathe out, say silently to yourself, "one."

5. Continue to breathe in and out, saying "one" on your out breath.

6. Notice how calm and relaxed you become.

7. Let yourself be ever calmer as you continue to breathe.

8. When you are ready, open your eyes and notice how calm and focused you feel.

Tip Number Two: Study Smarter, Not Harder

Use these techniques to prepare. You will be surprised at what a difference it will make.

1. *Avoid cramming for the test.* Don't kid yourself and try to master too much information the night before the test. It won't work, and it can leave you feeling even more anxious.

2. *Master the main concepts first,* so you will have a context for the details.

3. *Try to anticipate the questions for the test,* and review your text, notes, and other readings to find the best answer.

4. *Remember to be actively engaged,* caring about what you are studying.

5. *Don't forget to speak your answers out loud to get your left-brain involved.*

Tip Number Three: Watch Your Attitude

Catch yourself if you are making more of the test than is good for you.

1. *Watch the drama.* Don't psyche yourself out by building up the importance of the test unrealistically.

2. *Monitor your self-talk.* If you catch that voice in your head worrying away, tell yourself, "I can worry later. Right now, my job is to get ready for the test."

3. *Avoid thinking about all the negative consequences if you don't do well.* (Your mother will not actually kill you.)

4. *Set an expectation that you will show what you know, doing your personal best.*

5. *Plan a reward you can give yourself after the test.* Give yourself a treat for doing your best. Don't wait for the grade to come back.

Tip Number Four: Take Care of Yourself

Don't forget what you need physically and emotionally in order to do your best.

1. *Get enough sleep* the night before the test. Being tired is never a good idea.

2. *Eat well the day of the test.* Watch your caffeine or energy drink consumption, as they can lead to the jitters. Sweets can raise and then drop your energy when you most need it.

3. *Try smart foods.* Nuts, string cheese, and raisins all help you stay alert and focused.

4. *Keep up your exercise.* Your head needs your body!

5. *Avoid anxiety-generating classmates.* Walk away. Far away.

Tip Number Five: Slow Down and Take the Test

If you follow these tips, you may feel like you are going too slowly. For a right-brain learner, that is a good thing. That will be a clue that you are focusing on the words and using your left brain.

1. *When you receive the test, take time to review all of it, reading the directions twice.* Don't assume you know what they say and skip over them.

2. *Do the easiest parts first.* Keep moving, and don't get frustrated if you don't know some of the questions. You don't have to be perfect.

3. *Watch your time.* Tell yourself how much time you have left when you look at the clock.

4. *Don't worry about classmates who leave before you do.* Remember to stay focused until the end of the test.

5. *Give yourself the reward you planned.* Relax and enjoy yourself.

STANDARDIZED TESTS

With the advent of standardized tests, both the MSAs and the HSAs, I frequently hear from puzzled parents. One mother called to say that her son was in AP Biology, and had a high A in the course. She was surprised to hear the school's recommendation that he attend an eight-week after-school prep course for the HSA. The reason? He didn't test well.

How does the Stressless Tests® study method that you are learning here help you with standardized tests? How is this method different from classes that may be offered in your school? While many schools offer special prep classes, the focus is usually on the structure and content of the test itself. *The material you are learning here in "What's My Style?" focuses on the other half of the test: you, the person taking it.*

Students in my Study Skills courses tell me they think of the MSA and the HSA as easy exams. They describe the exam as one that would be almost impossible to fail. So, what's the hard part? "It's the environment," they say. "Everything is different from the usual test." We know by now that the impact of stress is an important factor in and of itself.

My students talk about the added pressures of knowing they have to pass the test, the expectations of their parents, and having someone other than their classroom teacher administer it. Sometimes, the wording on tests is different from the way they have learned the material in class.

Experience has shown that once you master the Stressless Tests® method, you will have greater confidence and higher performance on all tests, including classroom and standardized tests.

Five Top Reasons for Failing a Test

Have you ever been surprised to find out you did poorly on a test that you thought you had aced? If you are like most students, you will be disappointed, and you won't know how to analyze where you went wrong. Use the tips below to analyze what went wrong and what corrective action you can take. *The important thing is to think about your test results in a way that will actually help your future performance.*

1. I didn't prepare for the test.

    • You may not have self-tested in advance and mistakenly thought you were ready. Don't skip that step.

    • Sometimes students make a conscious choice to forgo preparation for a quiz or a minor test if they already have a good grade in the class and need the time for other projects or studies. If so, be prepared to accept the lower grade as a natural consequence of your decision, and don't stress over it.

2. I didn't remember I had a test.

• Don't treat this as a memory problem. Right-brain thinkers tend to rely on memory more than is realistic.

• Instead, focus on your organizational skills, find a consistent place to write it down, and be sure to review your assignments every day. List all assignments, deadlines, tests, etc.

3. I didn't study the right material.

• Clarify with your teachers in advance what material is to be covered and what type of test you will be taking, even if you think you know.

4. I never really understood the material.

> • If not, you need to take action to support yourself in mastering the material. You may need to be more focused in the class (it is easy to drift off if confused), ask questions, ask for time with the teacher outside of class, or find someone who can help you. Consider whether there is a classmate, a friend, family member, or a tutor who can help. *Ask them what a picture of the concept would look like.*

5. I understood the material but froze during the test.

> • *Some anxiety before a test is normal, and actually provides a boost of energy.* If the freeze response has become a recurring problem, it may be your habitual physical response to stress, and you may need to develop skills to overcome it. If so, review Tip Number One in the Test Anxiety Tips section.

TEST PREPERATION PRIORITIES GUIDE

Use this table to help set your study priorities for your exams. By thinking through in advance how to allocate your time, you will feel less stressed. Fill in the chart, resisting the impulse to keep it all in your head. It helps to see it.

First, list each subject and the day of the test. Fill in your current grade. Next, think about how challenging each course is for you, and rate it high, medium or low. Then look at each subject and assign a rating for your priority for study. For example, if you already have an A in a subject that is very easy for you, you will not need to put in as much time preparing for the exam. That subject would be rated a low priority for study. For subjects in which you want to pull up the grade, or for those that you find more difficult to understand, you will want to assign a higher priority. Those with the highest priority will need the most time.

Once you have assigned priorities, use the Help Needed column to prompt you to think about the courses in which you need more help to prepare for the exam. Jot down the resources you need, whether it is help from parents, teachers, your textbooks, the internet, tutors, etc. Then be sure to follow up to get the help you need.

SUBJECT	TEST DAY	GRADE	LEVEL OF DIFFICULTY HIGH, MEDIUM, LOW	STUDY PRIORITY HIGH, MEDIUM, LOW	HELP NEEDED

Multiple Choice Tests: 10 Strategies for Success

Before you start your test, remember to do some deep breathing to relax. It will help you concentrate and do you best.

1. Read the whole question carefully.

    *   Don't skip any words or assume you know what it says. Read it all.

2. Read all the choices before you select one.

    *   Let yourself think about each one. It is just as likely to be the last answer as it is to be the first answer.

3. Anticipate the answer and look for the one you expect to find.

    *   If you don't find what you are looking for, choose the best one available.

4. Cross out all choices you know are incorrect.

   • This will help you focus on the correct answer.

5. Look for choices that use the same words used by your teacher or your textbook.

   • This is usually the correct answer.

6. Look for words such as *all, always,* and *never.*

   • These answers are usually incorrect. Stop and think it through.

7. Look for hints to answers in other items on the test.

   • Sometimes the answer is found in a different statement or question.

8. Choose "all of the above" only if you are certain that all choices are correct.

   • If just one of the choices is incorrect, then "all of the above" is not the correct answer.

9. Choose "none of the above" only if you are certain that all of the choices are *incorrect*.

   - If just one of the answers is correct, do not choose "none of the above."

10. Don't change your answer unless you are sure that a different answer is better.

    - Don't over think or take a wild guess. Often, your first choice is correct.

Essay Test Tips: Preparation

This is a left-brain, structured task. You do not want to wing it during an essay exam.

The main reason students fail essay tests is not because they cannot write but because they fail to answer the questions fully and specifically, and because their answer is not well organized.

To succeed, you need to structure your thinking in advance. As you prepare, carefully organize and prioritize the major content areas in writing. Focus on your key sources for the test: your class notes, study guide, or textbook. Be sure you clarify with your teacher the material that will be covered. *It's better to understand and know a few things very well than to have a large quantity of unorganized, poorly learned material.*

Essay exams may include either short answer questions or long, general questions. These exams have no one specific answer that you are expected to remember. You will be asked to state your opinion, based on the information you have covered in the course.

Five Steps to Successful Preparation

- List all topics that you know are going to be on the test, along with their subtopics. Use this as your study guide.
- Skim all the materials to be covered, and note the ones that need additional study.
- Read or reread all materials you have not understood.
- Write down all the key topics covered in class and in your reading.
- Develop a series of written groups of information for each topic. Find the natural categories suggested by the material. Categories that may be useful include "who," "what," "when," "where," "how it works," "key characteristics," "cause and effect," and "examples."

Taking the Essay Test

Remember to let yourself be focused, slowing down to read and absorb the directions.

1. Read all the directions and questions thoroughly.

    • Note the number of items, points per question, range of difficulty, and time available.

    • Jot down any immediate answers that come to your mind, such as lists, outlines, etc. Write down any other key information you think you might forget.

2. Analyze the test question and divide it into its main parts and subparts.

    • Quickly construct a rough outline.

    • Note the instructions included in the question; e.g., compare or contrast.

    • Use the outline as a "map" to answer the essay question. If you don't have time to finish the whole test, this outline may give you some points. Most important, the outline will help you to stay focused.

3. Make your answer as specific as possible.

   • First, answer only what you are asked.

   • Be specific, and avoid generalities.

4. Use part of the test question in your answer at the beginning of the paragraph. This signals to the reader that you are answering this part of the essay here and will earn you points.

5. Include an introductory statement at the beginning and a summary paragraph at the end.

6. Review your answers. Your essay is written under the intensity of a deadline, but it is graded under much more relaxed conditions. Allow yourself sufficient time at the end to check for spelling, grammar, omitted words, incorrect dates, etc.

Right Brain Essays

He is a pre-eminent figure in his field, whose work has helped people around the world. His credentials are from the best universities, and his work is supported by some of the most prestigious organizations in the country. I was excited to have a chance to be with him at a two-day presentation in Washington. With high anticipation, I gathered along with about three hundred other professionals, expecting to come away with cutting edge information I could use in my own work. Then, I sat through his first day of lecturing and was stunned. True, he gave the latest research results, videos from programs around the world, and an occasional hint of the practices found most effective.

The problem? They were all presented in a random order, leaving us confused and upset. He never made the tie between the research, the insider politics, and the practices. We were left dangling, with no way to know whether the practices he mentioned were supported by the research. It was impossible to know how to apply the information to our own work. He was in the process of alienating all of us.

Have you ever gotten similar feedback on your short essay exams? That "it needs to be better organized." Or that "your conclusions are not supported by the facts." It can be frustrating feedback, especially if you don't know any other way to work.

So, what's the problem and what's the solution? The problem is that right-brain thinkers tend to generate their answers in random order. Answers don't arrive in a neat, sequential, cause and effect package. They arrive in discrete, often unrelated modules. So, first, you need to know this: Don't expect it to be different. Let it be just fine.

What to do? First, be clear in your intent. What question are you trying to answer? Then, realize that you need to take the random pieces of information and organize them. After they arrive. Show the relationship of each piece of information. Are they all examples of the main point? Is there a cause and effect relationship? Did they take place on a timeline? It isn't hard. Usually you can make the links with one or two sentences, providing the context. Then, make sure to put the information in order in a way that flows for ease of understanding. It is an art form, and you can do it. It is just like organizing the pieces in a puzzle. With a little practice, you will master it.

Essay Test Terms Glossary

ANALYZE: Break the question into the main separate parts and then discuss, examine, or interpret each part.

COMMENT: When asked to comment, you are asked to explore the impact and meaning of something. Your response should cover an explanation, criticism, or an illustration of something written or said.

COMPARE: Examine qualities or characteristics of two or more things in order to discover similarities and differences. Usually, comparisons ask for similarities more than differences.

CONTRAST: Tell how two or more topics are different from each other.

CRITICIZE, INTERPRET, and REVIEW: Express your judgment with respect to the correctness or merits of the factors under consideration. Give the results of your own analysis and discuss the limitations and positive points of the work.

DEFINE: Definitions call for concise, clear, authoritative meanings. Details are not required.

DIAGRAM and ILLUSTRATE: Present a drawing chart, plan, or graphic representation in your answer. You may be expected to label the diagram or add a brief explanation or description.

DISCUSS: Examine, analyze carefully, and present detailed considerations for and against. Compare and contrast. This direction is often found in essay tests.

EVALUATE: Present a careful appraisal of the problem, stressing both advantages and limitations. You may cite an expert by name, or give your own opinion.

EXPLAIN, RELATE: Clarify and interpret the material you present. State the "how" or "why," reconcile differences in opinion or experimental results, and state causes, if possible. In brief, tell how it all happened.

JUSTIFY, PROVE: To justify your answer, provide factual evidence or logical reasons, especially those presented in class or your text. Present your evidence in a convincing form.

LIST, ENUMERATE: List several ideas, events, things, reasons, etc. Be concise.

OUTLINE: Give the main points, omitting minor details, and present the information in a systematic arrangement. You do not need to do a formal outline based on Roman numerals or letters.

SUMMARIZE: Give the main points or facts in condensed form, including conclusions. Omit details, illustrations, and examples.

TRACE: Show the order of events, or give a description of historical sequence, development of events, or the progress of a subject.

STUDY TIPS

Find the "So That..."

If you are reading this book, chances are you

>are often impatient,

>don't like to waste your time,

>and quickly get bored with seemingly meaningless tasks.

Most likely, you

>are frequently disappointed with tests results when you

>thought you had studied enough, and

>find it hard to settle down to study or do homework.

Sitting in a lecture that you don't find interesting, you will get bored—and then do whatever you usually do when you get bored. Daydream. Text a friend while hiding the phone. Disrupt the class. Make a joke. Talk to the student next to you. Why? Because it is a way for you to get involved again, on your own terms.

What's missing for you is any lively *reason* for you to settle down, tune in, or pay attention. You haven't stopped to think about your "so that...." Meaning, you haven't checked in to see what makes it important for *you*, so you have automatically blown it off. You will be surprised to learn how much difference it makes when you find your own reasons.

What's a "so that..."look like? Here are some examples.

1. I am going to tune in and pay attention in class, *so that*

- I can actually understand what this unit is about

- I can bring up my grade on my next test

- I can do my homework more quickly, without having to read through the text again

- I can contribute something positive to the class

- I can stop getting in trouble.

2. I am going to ask a question in class when I start getting lost, *so that*

- it is easier to pay attention

- I don't have to figure it out on my own later

- I don't get so bored!

3. I am going to speak out loud when I study, *so that*

- I get my left brain involved

- I will be better prepared for a test, and

- I will know when I have studied enough and can stop.

In summary, take action. Find your own reason to tune in. Put it in words, even if it is just in your own mind. You will still be getting involved on your own terms. And it sure beats sinking into boredom.

Challenges and Solutions Worksheet

Some challenges seem insurmountable. You are bored. You feel like you never have enough time. You can't stay focused in class. You don't understand math, and you think the teacher doesn't like you. You do well in class, but then fail the tests.

You may just take these things for granted, as though nothing you can do would make a difference. That, of course, is simply not true. That line of thinking leads to passive acceptance instead of active engagement of the issue. You can be proactive, and it *will* make a difference.

Start by listing your Challenges. Leave the Solutions column blank for the moment. You will find it empowering to name the issues, and to know that they are simply problems for which there are solutions. Know that it is really not about you, just the kinds of issues many students face. Come back to this page and fill in the Solutions as you come across them in other parts

of the book. Stay curious, and remember to be proactive.

MY STUDY CHALLENGES	SOLUTIONS

CHALLENGES AND SOLUTIONS WORKSHEET

Here are some examples of the kinds of solutions you may find.

Remember to find those that work for you.

STUDY CHALLENGES	SOLUTIONS
Math	Ask the teacher what the concept looks like as a picture
Focusing	Choose to stay engaged
Boredom	Study in blocks with breaks
Note taking	Use the Cornell method
Time pressure	Set priorities, and use a timer to keep track of time
Test pressure	Learn to prepare so I have confidence in myself

I have no special talents,

I am passionately curious.

Albert Einstein

Boredom: No Victims Allowed

It would be nice if you would leave, Albert. Your behavior at school, so distracted and absentminded, and your poor interest in all I teach set a bad example for the whole class.
–Teacher's comment to Albert Einstein as a child

There came a day when I just lost it in class, blurting out something that stunned me. Usually, I choose my words with care, both in class and out. I know that words can sting, alienating people in a moment. The last thing I want to do is turn someone off by speaking carelessly.

The class was a High School Study Skills class. And they were great. They were open, honest, and ready to take part in everything I suggested. Sitting in the back corner were three guys, who quickly became friends. Their common bond was the boredom they felt in their regular classes. As we worked through the classes on Intent, Learning Style, Focusing, and

Challenges and Solutions, they seemed to get the point, but they always reverted to proclamations of how boring school is. They were stuck.

Finally, it was the last day of class, and I was both determined to make a difference and perplexed as to how to help them get unstuck. I was standing next to one of the three when he said again that he got bored in class. I was amazed to hear the words, which then came tumbling out of my mouth: *"But you don't get to play victim to your own boredom! You can't use that as an excuse to not be involved!"*

My inner astonishment and regret was interrupted by a simultaneous gasp from all three of the boys. "Oh," said Ryan, *"that's* what I have been doing!" "Me, too!" said the other two. That was pretty much all it took, as all three said they just needed to stop feeling like they were somehow doomed to boredom. "Well, I'm not doing that anymore!" was their final word on the subject.

Outsmarting the Top 10 Stumbling Blocks to Studying

Stumbling Block #1: I Don't Know Where to Start

Your action step: take control. You just need to find a way to focus on the individual tasks, instead of the whole assignment. Bring in your left brain: that's what it does best. Make a written list of all the things you have to do. Then break your workload down into manageable chunks. Set your priorities, paying attention to due dates and tests.

Stumbling Block #2: I've Got So Much to Study . . . And So Little Time

Your action step: preview and sort the topics. Survey your study guide, reading material, and notes. Identify the most important topics emphasized and areas still not understood. Previewing saves time by helping you organize and focus in on the main topics.

Stumbling Block #3: This Stuff Is So Dry, I Can't Even Stay Awake Reading It

Your action step: get engaged! Set your intent to be actively involved with the text as you read. Ask yourself, "What is important to remember about this section?" Take notes or underline key concepts using color highlighters. Get your left-brain language center involved by discussing the material with others in your class. Stay on the offensive, especially with material that you don't find interesting, rather than "eye reading."

Stumbling Block #4: I Read It. I Understand It. But I Just Can't Get It to Sink In

Your action step: integrate the new material with what you already know. We remember best the things that are most meaningful to us. As you are reading, build on the new information with your own examples. Try to put the new material in your own words. You will be able to remember it better if you can link it to something that's already meaningful to you.

78

Stumbling Block #9: Cramming Before a Test Helps Keep It Fresh in My Mind

Your action step: space out your studying. Start studying now. Keep studying as you go along. Begin with an hour or two a day about one week before the exam, and then increase study time as the exam approaches. Recall increases as study time gets spread out over time. Cramming can lead to material being stored in your short-term memory, where it will be forgotten once the test is over.

Stumbling Block #10: I'm Gonna Stay Up All Night 'til I Get This

Your action step: avoid mental exhaustion. Everything is worse with sleep deprivation. Take short breaks often when you are studying. Before a test, make sure you have a well-rested mind. When you take a study break, and when you go to sleep at night, take your mind off your studies. Relax and unwind, mentally and physically. It's more important than ever to take care of yourself before an exam! Eat well, sleep, and get enough exercise.

Getting Organized: Think Like a Chef

Carley described her typical evening of getting ready to do her homework. First, she sat down at her desk, and then she had to get up to find a pen that had ink in it. Next, she realized she had forgotten to get her textbook out of her backpack, and had to go retrieve it. Then, she needed a cold drink. Next, it was her iPod. Finally, she realized she didn't have the worksheet she was going to fill out. "At that point," she said, "I just gave up in frustration and went off to watch television." Sound familiar?

Contrast that experience to the celebrity chefs we see on the Food Network. If the recipe calls for one third of a cup of grated cheese, they reach over and pick up a little bowl that magically already has that exact amount of grated cheese. Awesome! Next, it is the milk, the salt and pepper, and the olive oil. It sure beats the way most of us cook, getting out each ingredient only when we are ready to use it. That's when we usually discover that we only have a quarter cup of milk when the recipe calls for a half cup.

If you apply the celebrity chef technique to your own supplies, you will have less frustration and enjoy getting things done in a lot less time. You can set up your system in three easy steps. One, make a list of all the supplies you would like to have at your fingertips. Be expansive. Include extra binders and dividers, several sheets of poster board, as well as pens, notebook and graph paper, legal pads, highlighters, Sharpies, ink for your computer, etc. Think it through. Then, go shopping at an office supply store. Pick out a pen that feels good in your hand and has ink that flows freely. Buy a box of them. Take advantage of all the great colors and designs, choosing items that you will enjoy looking at. Buy quantities of everything so you don't run out the night before your project is due. Think about whether you need an organizer box to keep everything together.

Finally, back home, find the right spot in which to store your own little mini-supply store. Make a place wherever you study, in a container that only you will use. It may be a desk drawer, a filing cabinet, or a shelf in your closet. Then, enjoy knowing you have plenty of whatever you may need, right at your fingertips.

THE BOREDOM POSTURE

Think about the way you sit in class when you are totally bored. Chances are, you have a particular posture when you are no longer engaged. Are you a lean-on-the back-of-your-chair-legs-with-your feet-on-the-bottom-rung-of-the-desk type, or do you prefer a bury-your-head-in-your-arms-on-your-desk approach? Or, perhaps you maintain eye contact with your teacher, a mask of interest firmly in place, while your mind is far away? Or...something else? I invite you to take a moment now and take that position, just so you make the connection of the posture and your feelings of boredom.

Whenever I invite my students to assume their boredom sitting position, they immediately know what it is and move into it. Then, I invite some of the students to come up front, look at the class, and ask them how they would like to try and teach that class. "I wouldn't!" is the usual response. That's when they discover that their own obvious display of detachment may make it even harder for the teacher to connect with them.

Try this. The next time you catch yourself in your bored position in class, shift out of it. Instead, sit up, lean forward, be attentive, and get involved. Above all, be curious. Ask questions, take notes, and maintain your focus. Studies have shown that students can actually affect the quality of classroom presentations by the level of their response. Simply put, studies show that teachers teach better to more engaged students.

Do your own experiment to see what difference it makes for you. See if you can enhance your feeling of connection, no matter what. Nobody likes to be bored!

No Place for Anything

There's an old saying about having a place for everything, and everything in its place. For right-brain thinkers, the challenge is to realize that you first need to *create* a place for all kinds of things. Usually, you are more likely to put something down "just for a minute" because there is no obvious place for it. It can be a problem. My advice is to take time to create your space in advance, before you need it. Make it a short, separate project to create a space for something you use all the time.

Christina is a good example of the right-brain approach. She once complained in class that her stepmother had just alphabetized all of her CDs, and now she couldn't find anything. When I asked her how she usually organized them, she cheerfully replied, "Wherever I can make a space, I just push them in."

Memory Strategies: BATBY GOB STOPL

Have you ever had the experience of forgetting your answer as you said it aloud in class, just when you were most confident you knew it? If so, you know how embarrassing it can be. So, just imagine having an obvious memory lapse in front of millions of people, fishing for a word and not being able to retrieve it. Such was the fate of Senator John McCain one Sunday morning on *Meet the Press* during his campaign for President. Having confidently announced that five previous Secretaries of State had endorsed him, he stalled after he named four of them. The moderator sat silently as Senator McCain tried, without success, to pull the last name out of his memory. Watching the clip as it replayed later, the commenter noted, "It's strange he didn't have some mnemonic device ready to help him remember them."

The strangely named mnemonic device (derived from the Latin for mindfulness) is quite simply a pattern of letters, words,

Try making up words or nonsense sayings to see if it is a natural skill you have. Some people have fun with it, and some find it easier to simply look at the list, say the words silently in their mind, and "just memorize it." Use whichever method is easiest for you.

If Your Teacher Locks You in the Closet

It was the last class, and Sean still had a challenge he hadn't figured out how to solve. "What do you do when you have a mean teacher?" he asked. The ensuing conversation went something like this.

"Any chance this mean teacher is a math or science teacher?" I asked.

Looking surprised, Sean answered, "He's my math teacher. And he is really mean to me!"

"Don't forget that we have talked about the fact that many math teachers are going to be left-brain thinkers. They may be more task-oriented than you are, and not be as personal. Is that what is going on?" I asked.

"No, he's really mean to me, and everyone else, too."

By now, others in the class joined in, agreeing that this one teacher was truly mean.

"So, what does he do to be mean to you?" I asked. "Yell at you? Put you down? Slap a ruler on your desk?"

Silence from Sean.

"Really, tell me what he is actually doing that makes him mean," I persisted.

"He makes me show my work on math tests," he blurted out.

"Okay," I tried again. "Remember, we know that even though you get the answers first, you do need to work back from there and show how you got there. It's a right brain thing, and, if you don't show your work, your teacher might get pretty frustrated with you, not knowing how you did it."

"But, it's so easy!" Sean protested. "Why do I have to show the work, when it is so obvious?"

From across the room, Zac called out, providing the last word on the subject. "If your math teacher locks you in the closet, then he's being mean! Otherwise, you just need to show your work!"

Well said, Zac.

A Script in Her Head

One of the great parts of my classes is having students reveal their discoveries of their unique abilities. Take Abi, who loves acting. As a right-brain learner with a photographic memory, she has discovered that she has a great advantage when it comes to learning her lines. One night in class, she described her system. First, she highlights her lines in the script. She then studies them, practicing with the rest of the cast. Her real advantage comes during the performances.

"When I'm onstage," she says, "I can visualize the page of the script so I can literally read right from it. Usually, the lines I see in my mind's eye are in the same color that I highlighted them with. That makes it so much easier than just memorizing them. So, for example, I just watch for the lines in red!"

THE SURPRISING HARVARD STUDY

When we think of Harvard students, we think they must be among the best and brightest. Very smart, very accomplished, and most likely very good at studying. But a study published by the Academic Skills Center at Dartmouth College offers a surprising insight. As reported, Dr. Perry, a psychologist and Director of the Harvard Reading-Study Center, gave 1500 first-year students a thirty-page chapter of a history book to read. He told them that they would have about twenty minutes to read the chapter. Then they would be asked to identify the important details and to write an essay on what they had read. It should be noted that there was a paragraph marked "Summary" that summarized the most important points. And, there were also notes in the margins.

Surprisingly, at the end of the time, only fifteen of the 1500 students were able to write a short statement on what the chapter was all about! That is just one percent of the total. When asked why they hadn't read the summary, or skimmed the notes in the margins, students said they felt that would be cheating! The researchers branded this approach to textbook reading as a waste of time, and as an example of "obedient purposelessness." Or, as my students have labeled it, an example of "eye reading."

Clearly, the missing skill is that of scanning a textbook, with an eye to what can be skipped and what is important. You can learn these skills now. You can have better textbook skills than those Harvard students. Read on.

Six Tips for Texts

If you enjoy reading for pleasure, or if you like a good movie, you know what it means to be engaged in the story. You enjoy thinking along with it, wondering and anticipating how it will turn out. Of course, the author or filmmaker has worked hard to make sure you are engaged and enjoying the experience. They want to have a successful book or movie that will sell well.

Most textbook producers are operating from a different perspective. They have not set out to engage you in the same way. There is no story line, and you are not immersed in the material, complete with great music and special effects. The trick then, is to learn how to get engaged with the material on your own.

Have you ever found yourself "eye reading," covering the assigned reading and then realizing you have no idea what you just read? Most students have that experience at one time or another. How do you solve it? Try the following six tips.

1. **Convert the reading from a monologue into a dialogue.** In a monologue, only one person speaks. In a dialogue, two or more people speak. In other words, don't be a passive recipient, just "listening" to the textbook. Your brain will not be able to absorb and integrate the material. Instead, make it a dialogue, with your brain actively involved. Talk back.

2. **Begin by skimming the book, noticing how the author draws your attention to the most important material.** Are there previews, summaries, or test questions and answers? Are there key words or notes in the margin? Is there bold face type, picture captions, or graphics to capture your attention? Next, read the introduction, the headings and subheadings, and all of the other highlighted text that you spot. Use any study guide or

set of questions your teacher has provided. Read with your purpose in the front of your mind.

3. **Focus on each subheading, turning it into a simple "who, what, why, when, or where" question.** This is your side of the dialogue. Be curious, even if it is not your favorite subject.

4. **Read the following details to see how it answers your questions.** Take time to hear the words in your mind as you read. Think through how it relates to other information you already know.

5. **Make the information yours.** Take notes, underline or highlight it, and then say it out loud. Use your own words to explain the main concepts. Explain it as you would in a class. This will get your left brain involved, and help you to be more test-ready.

6. **Review.** Read your notes, the chapter summaries, and the other material you found as you scanned the chapter. Read it with the goal of mastering the material and being able to explain it in your own words. Reread it from time to time, taking in more and more of both the big picture and the details. It is surprising how much books seem to change as we understand them better.

TIME
MANAGEMENT

How Much Time Do You Have?

Do you ever feel pressured by time? Many students do. There are two types of time stress. One is the feeling of, "I never have enough time." The other involves knowing you have plenty of time, but feeling that you still never get the things done that you want to do.

You will find it helpful to see how much free time you actually have each day. To convert your feelings into facts. To help you gain a better picture of your time, try the following. See if you can get 24 one-dollar bills. Hold them in one hand. Imagine that each dollar equals an hour. The dollar bills in your hand stand for the 24 hours you have to spend every day. Each day, you start fresh with another 24 hours. Think of it this way: you have as much time as Bill Gates. No one can create more time. All you can do is spend what you have in a clear and focused way. Now, let's find out where your time goes.

- On the "How Do I Spend My Time?" table, start by filling in three categories of how you use your time.

- First, find the time you go to bed during the week and draw a line across the box on top of that number.

- Next, draw a line for the time you get up on school days. Label the boxes Sleep.

- Now, draw the lines for the time you leave home for school in the morning, and the time you leave school.

- Label the box School.

- Make boxes for each regularly scheduled, supervised activity you have during the school week. This might include sports, music lessons, jobs, or religious education classes, etc. (This does not include homework, hanging out with friends, video games, etc.)

• Look at your chart and choose your busiest day. Count the number of empty boxes between the end of school and bedtime. Write this number at the top of the chart where it says, "Busy days _____hours." (If several days are equally busy, choose one of them to count.)

• Choose your least busy day, and count the empty boxes between the end of school and bedtime. Record the number at the top of the chart where it says, "Easy days _____ hours."

• With these two numbers, you now have the range of how many hours you have available to spend. Note how many hours are already committed for you.

How Do I Spend My Time?

Busy days _____ hours Easy days _____ hours

	Monday	Tuesday	Wednesday	Thursday	Friday
12 midnight					
1 am					
2					
3					
4					
5					
6					
7					
8					
9					
10					
11					
12 noon					

HOW MUCH TIME DO YOU HAVE?

	Monday	Tuesday	Wednesday	Thursday	Friday
1 pm					
2					
3					
4					
5					
6					
7					
8					
9					
10					
11					

Tips For Time Management

If you are a creative, intuitive, right-brain learner, the idea of managing time can seem like a mysterious and sometimes impossible undertaking. Keeping track of time is not a task that comes naturally. From the brain's point of view, there is a built-in clock only in the left hemisphere, while the right side of the brain goes about its business happily oblivious of the passing of time.

The good news is that you can see time in a whole new way, and learn how to be in charge of the ways in which you spend it. You will find out how good it feels to get things done faster and easier.

Tip Number 1: Identify your personal best time for studying. Are you a "morning person" or a "night person?" Do you wake up fresh and mentally sharp? Or do you prefer to stay up late, and then get a slower start in the morning? Everyone naturally has high and low periods of attention and concentration, so use it to your advantage. Use your most focused and alert times to study. If, for example, you are a night person, don't even think of getting up extra early for the final test prep. It's not going to happen.

Tip Number 2: Study difficult subjects first. When your mind is sharp, you can process information more quickly with less effort. You will save time and get an energy boost knowing the hardest part is finished.

Tip Number 3: Study in shorter time blocks with short breaks. Don't try to push yourself to keep studying long after you have lost focus. Be honest with yourself about how long you can stay focused, actively engaged, and taking in information. It may be 15 minutes, or it may be a half hour. Study for that block of time, then take a 5-minute break. Time your break with something that will beep or ring to let you know time is up.

You will be less tired and waste a lot less time. Remember, it's all about blocks and breaks.

Tip Number 4: Make sure your surroundings are conducive to studying. Choose a distraction-free area, or create your own. This includes all tempting electronic media, from your cell phone to your television and computer. If you need to create your space, make it a separate activity. Give yourself 15 minutes to think it through and change the space. Then take a break.

Tip Number 5: Make time for entertainment and relaxation. You need to have a social life and you need to have a balance in your life. Make it a priority to have down time. Resist getting over scheduled.

Tip Number 6: Make sure you have time to sleep and eat properly. Have you ever found yourself using sleep as your time management "bank?" When you need a few extra hours for studying or socializing, you withdraw a few hours of sleep. The problem with this is that it makes the time you spend studying less effective. When you are tired, you will need a couple of hours of clock time to get an hour of productive time. Sleep deprivation makes everything harder, from sports to studies.

Go With Your Flow

If you have a crowded schedule, it is important to know which activities re-energize you. To find out what works best for you, take a moment and jot down all of your typical after school and evening activities. Don't leave anything out.

Your list will probably include such activities as homework, sports, dinner, watching television, hanging out with friends, working out, school activities, social networking, video games, doing nothing, reading, going to the mall, etc. Put everything on the list, with an estimate of how much time you might spend on each in a given day. Be honest, even if it means you are logging in many hours in front of the television, or playing video games. List everything.

Next, think about what your ideal schedule would be if you could arrange it any way you want. For example, are you someone who needs to socialize or do something physically active after school? Or would you prefer to get your homework and studying done first? Now, rearrange the activities in the order in which you would prefer to do them. Start by writing down your ideal bedtime. Do you want to get to bed by 10? Write it down. Next, put down all of your activities with the actual clock time. (If you spend 2 hours in sports, for example, is it from 3:00 to 5:00? Or 2:00 to 4:00?) Chances are, you will need to make decisions about where to cut some time in order to get to bed on time. Look at your list carefully, and choose the activities and time that work best for you.

Put your schedule into practice, and see what a difference it makes.

My Brain Just Died

He was a bright and motivated student, whose favorite place to study was the dining room table. He was also a sociable guy. Somehow, in the midst of family discussions, dinner preparations in the kitchen, and his favorite music, he could study at his best. He liked to talk things through as he studied, and I enjoyed helping him. I would ask questions, and he would tell me what he knew.

Strangely enough, at a certain point in the evening, he suddenly couldn't answer the questions anymore. Without warning, he was done. We were both curious about how it happened. As it turned out, it always happened at almost exactly nine o'clock at night.

Once we saw the pattern, it became a standing joke. "Oops, my brain just died. It must be nine o'clock!" So we stopped. Or started earlier.

Sound familiar? Know your own patterns, and don't fight them. Just let them be true, and plan around them.

Masters of Procrastination

If we hurry, we can still be late!

Definition: Procrastination: put off doing something that needs to be done

I always enjoy the stories students tell when I ask, "Who is really good at procrastinating? Truly a master?" Almost everyone in class has a hand up, vying to tell their story. The examples quickly escalate. Do these sound familiar?

"I always put my homework off to the last minute the night before."

"I do mine on the bus."

"I do it in the class before it is due."

"I have a split class with lunch in the middle, so I do it at lunch."

"I did my entire science fair project the night before it was due, and got an A+ for creativity!"

"I put off doing a project and then forgot about it. During the class in which it was due, I used my cell phone, googled the information, and wrote it up on the spot!"

Damian, a high school student, said he was so good at procrastinating that he is thinking of turning pro!

With so many right-brain students in my classes, it is no wonder that talking about procrastination is a guaranteed source of lively conversation. Almost everyone recognizes this as a personal habit. They also recognize its down side. "It is kind of stressful to have something hanging over your head, especially long-term assignments," is a common comment. Also, students say they don't learn as much as they do when they are putting their full effort into a project. Plus, there is the pressure from parents, who want them to stop procrastinating.

Left-brain students tend to look on in bewilderment. They say they simply get on with it, doing what they need to do without putting it off.

As it turns out, most students don't understand why they put things off. Or, as middle-schooler Eric asked, "So how come I say I am going to do something, but then I don't? How does that work?"

The Simple Secret

Here is how it works. Don't forget that the right brain is connected to your feelings. One of its jobs is to keep you in touch with what you are feeling. Think for a minute about what that voice in your head says when you focus on something you don't want to do, whether it is homework or emptying the dishwasher. How about, "Yeah, I don't really feel like it right now. I'll do it later." Sound familiar? In the pure right-brain realm, it is all about feelings. Plus, without a sense of time passing, the right brain always feels like there is more time. You therefore tell yourself, "I don't feel like doing it right now, and besides, there is still plenty of time!"

Focusing is being all in one place
at one time

Focusing means simultaneously
thinking about and caring about
what you are doing in the very
moment you are doing it.

Solving Your Procrastination: Why do you do it?

How do you get beyond procrastinating? What do you do with that little voice that just wants to put things off? Take a look at some of the reasons why you may be procrastinating. Highlight those points you find most helpful.

Why do you procrastinate? Take a glance at this list, and read those that apply to you.

- *You may feel overwhelmed by the task.* (Note that "overwhelmed" is a feeling.) In response, you avoid it. You may put off your studies (especially long-term projects), and spend more time with friends, video games, or social activities. Or, you may simply worry more, or feel stuck, without knowing how to move ahead. Sometimes, you just give in to your feelings, and give up on the work at hand.

- *You may not be clear on your priorities.* Under stress, you may feel that you have too much to do, so there is no sense trying. Or, just as likely, you will tell yourself that you have plenty of time later, so there is no point in starting now. (And we know the right brain doesn't have a sense of time, so it will always think there is more time, even if you are totally scheduled.) Either way, what you are missing is a clear sense in your own mind of what specific tasks you need to do, and when exactly you will do it.

- *You may have difficulty focusing.* When you start to do your homework, you spend your time daydreaming, staring into space, or thinking about your boyfriend or girlfriend. You may go off into a fantasy world, instead of being in reality.

- *Your study environment is distracting, disorganized, and noisy.* You may try to do your homework or study with the television on. (Bad idea!) Or you keep running around to get the book you need, your iPod, another pen or pencil, or a snack. Or, you check on every text message or answer your cell phone. You may sit or lie on your bed to study, and then fall asleep.

- *You are feeling fear and anxiety.* You may be worried about getting a failing grade, or have given up on even understanding a class. Then, you spend more time worrying about your projects, papers, and exams than you do working on them.

- *You may fall into negative belief patterns, where you undercut yourself.* "I'll never learn this," or "I just don't have what it takes," or "My parents are going to kill me if I don't do well," are typical self-defeating statements.

- *You may have real and difficult personal problems to deal with.* Family financial worries, illness in the family, or a parent or sibling serving in a dangerous part of the world may take a toll on you.

• *You may have unrealistic expectations or be a perfectionist.* Out of anxiety, you may over-prepare. Perhaps you think you have to read everything ever written on a topic before you can even start your paper. Or, you do your project, but worry it is not your best, and so it is not good enough to hand in. (We know that some of the world's great artists, including Monet, frequently destroyed his paintings, thinking they weren't good enough. Imagine what has been lost to the world.)

Solving Your Procrastination: How to Get Over It

Tip Number One: Set Your Intent

• Stop, think, and make a conscious decision about what you want to do. Put it into words, if only in your own mind.

Tip Number Two: Set Your Priorities and Outcomes

• Think about, and jot down, what you need to do first. Name the benefit to you that you want to achieve. For example, "I am going to study for tomorrow's quiz until I feel confident that I know the material. I want to get an A on the quiz."

Tip Number Three: Break Big Assignments into Smaller Pieces

• For a long-term assignment, write down the major parts that are involved. For example, for a research paper, it might involve choosing the topic, research, drafting an outline, writing, and final editing. Then, choose one part to focus on at a time.

Tip Number Four: Name Self-Defeating Patterns and Move On

• It helps to be aware of the things that are holding you back. Name them so you can be in control. If you can say, "Oh, I'm just being a perfectionist again!" you can let it go and get to work.

Tip Number Five: Turn Distractions into Rewards

• Do you find yourself thinking about checking your text messages or stopping for a snack instead of studying? Great. Use them as rewards. Tell yourself, "As soon as I finish this task, I will get a snack." Then do it.

Time Tricks

Try this. Stop and think about what time it is right now. Don't look at a clock, your watch, or your cell phone. Instead, let the image of a clock appear to you in your mind's eye. Now, check and see how close you were. Close?

For many right-brainers, this is easy. Normal. Do you also wake up a moment or two before your alarm goes off? If so, just know these are right-brain skills. It is the right brain's way of tapping into time.

On the other hand, if you are a right-brain learner, you are probably really bad at predicting how long it will take you to do something. The paper you thought would take you a half-hour to write ends up taking two hours.

The truth is, the right brain has no sense of the passing of time. Think of it this way: only one side of the brain has a built-in clock. That's the left side. That's the side that focuses on how long it takes to go somewhere, or whether you have planned more than you can possibly accomplish.

It's amazing, isn't it? The right side of the brain knows what time it is, but not how long things take!

How to Be On Time

I was teaching a parents' workshop as part of a Saturday Math Academy for elementary and middle school students. As it turned out, almost all of the parents were right-brain learners. They loved learning about themselves, and we quickly developed a great rapport. We kidded and laughed a lot.

The program coordinator for the Math Academy, however, announced that she had tested as a left-brain learner. (No surprise there. This is math we're talking about.) So, when we discussed procrastination, she listened in astonishment to all the tales of people being late, putting things off, etc.

"Well," she said, "I'm never late. In fact, I'm usually early!" There was a moment of stunned silence as people took that in. Then someone asked, "How is that even possible? I mean just how do you do it?"

In a matter of fact manner, she said she thought about how long it would take to drive somewhere, then added in extra time, and left early. She explained this as though it was perfectly obvious. The response from the right-brainers was instantaneous. "But," they protested, you're wasting time!" "Think how much more you could get done if you didn't leave early!"

It's all about relating to time. Each side of the brain does it, but in very different ways.

Deadlines or No Deadlines?

Dan Ariely, author of *Predictably Irrational,* carried out an ingenious study in procrastination with his college students when he was a professor at MIT. On the first day of class, he announced that there would be three main papers due over the 12-week semester. The papers would largely determine course grades. Then he told students in one class that he had set no deadlines for the papers, and that they could hand them in any time they wanted during the semester. However, by the end of the first week of class, students needed to choose and commit to a deadline of their choice for each paper. They had complete freedom of choice, and could choose to space them out, or to hand them all in at the end of the course.

Once set, the deadlines could not be changed. Any papers handed in late would be penalized for each day they were late. No extra credit would be given for any papers handed in early. None of the papers would be graded until the end of the semester.

In a second class, he told students they could hand in their papers at any time during the semester as long as they were in by the last class. Unlike the first class, they did not need to set and commit to a deadline in advance, so there was no penalty involved for handing them in late.

In the third class, the professor assigned the deadlines for the fourth, eighth, and twelfth weeks, with no options and no flexibility. His study focused on which groups would achieve the best grades.

Given these three choices, which one would you pick? From your experience with procrastination, which group do you think got the best grades?

It turned out that students given the firm deadlines got the highest grades, those who had no deadlines at all did the worst, and those who set their own deadlines in advance were in the middle. His conclusion is that the best response to procrastination is to set inflexible deadlines for the students, at intervals that would allow them to do their best work. Those students who didn't space their deadlines realistically tended to wait until late in the semester, and then their work was rushed and not well done.

Consider this the next time you have a long-term project without interim deadlines. Try experimenting with making up your own well-spaced interim deadlines that allow you to do your best work. Then, stick to them.

WHAT'S THEIR STYLE?

J.K. ROWLING

"...as soon as I knew what writers were, I wanted to be one. I've got the perfect temperament for a writer; perfectly happy alone in a room, making things up."

J.K. Rowling

It's important to realize that the right brain is NOT simply a left brain that can't get it together. In fact, right-brain thinkers have an astoundingly different way of processing information. We might even say a wondrous way.

Consider J. K. Rowling, the world-renowned author of the Harry Potter series. As she describes it, "It was after a weekend's flat- (apartment) hunting, when I was travelling (sic) back to London on my own on a crowded train, that the idea for Harry Potter *simply fell into my head.*" (It has been reported that she was staring out the window at some cows chewing their cud in the field at the time.) She watched the images play out like a movie in her head. She says,

"I had been writing almost continuously since the age of six but I had never been so excited about an idea before. To my immense frustration, I didn't have a functioning pen with me, and I was too shy to ask anybody if I could borrow one. I think, now, that this was probably a good thing, because I simply sat and thought, for four (delayed train) hours, and all the details bubbled up in my brain, and this scrawny, black-haired, bespectacled boy who didn't know he was a wizard became more and more real to me. I think that perhaps if I had had to slow down the ideas so that I could capture them on paper I might have stifled some of them (although sometimes I do wonder, idly, how much of what I imagined on that journey I had forgotten by the time I actually got my hands on a pen)." She began to write the *Philosopher's Stone* that night.

It then took her over seven years to write the story she'd received in four hours. She has now become a billionaire, and has been recognized by *Time* magazine for the social, moral, and political inspiration she has given to the world.

This gives us a great example of a right-brain thinker. Notice the characteristics of the right brain at work:

- It receives information instantaneously.
- It feels as though no time passes, or that this somehow takes place outside of time.
- The information arrives in pictures, not words.
- It is exciting.
- The whole picture arrives at once, not in bits and pieces.
- The processing is so fast, it slows things down to write out the words.

Sound familiar? Great. The more you are aware of how you process information, the more you can take advantage of it. (Suppose, for example, J.K. Rowling had simply dismissed the information that "fell into her head"? What a horrible thought.) So, stay tuned in to your pictures.

NFL Head Coach: Is Football a Left-Brain Game?

We were discussing sports in class one day when one of the boys spontaneously observed, "Football must be a left-brain game. Quarterbacks wear a list of all the plays on a card on their wrist. They don't get to just make it up as they go along." It was a new thought, and it was fun to think about sports as either left- or right-brain games. So, I was especially interested when I came across a feature on Jim Zorn, the Head Coach of the Washington Redskins, in the Sports section of the *Washington Post*. Zorn is known for calling plays that surprise even his own players, and frequently confound the opposition. Redskins' players say they often have no idea what play he will call in any given moment. I began to wonder whether he was a random thinker—a right-brain coach in a left-brain game. As it turns out, it is more complicated than that.

Zorn holds a white laminated card on the sidelines. It is the one he uses to shield his mouth, so the opposing team can't read his lips. On the card are a series of plays, organized by an amazing variety of situations. There is a whole section of plays for the third down, another for short yardage, and another for when the team is closing in on the goal line. Even that is subdivided into 5-yard increments. There are plays to be run between the 15- and 20-yard line, between the 10 and 15, etc. It is tightly organized, so he doesn't have to search around for a play.

With everything scripted out, how does Zorn manage to surprise his own players?

Wide receiver Santana Moss is quoted as saying, "Sometimes we get in the huddle, and Jason calls the play, and we're like, 'Dang.'" As it turns out, Zorn considers not only the play coming up, but also the play after that, and what happens if it doesn't work. What happens if it does? He has the next four or five plays in his head at any given moment. He is clear on where he wants to go.

So, is this an analytical process? Left-brain all the way? Or is it based on intuition? What about his confidence in calling a play, even when it is unconventional? Or the smile his players describe? Clinton Portis describes it like this: "When (Zorn) calls a play and starts smiling like, 'This is it. This is the play right here. I'm telling you this is going to happen, and this is where we are going,' it's like, he really knows his stuff. It's exciting."

What do you think? Is it all analysis? Or is it a left-brain structure, with the right brain making the decisions? You decide.

Mozart's Magic

Wolfgang Amadeus Mozart is considered by some to be one of the greatest composers of all time. How did he do such brilliant work? You will recognize his amazing talents as those of an intuitive, or right-brain learner, who knew how to use his unusual skills. Mozart often experienced music that "fell into his head," just as J.K. Rowling describes her experience of receiving the story of Harry Potter. Joseph Chilton Pearce tells us that once Mozart had received a commission to write a piece of music, he would simply hold the commission in his mind, but not seek to write the music. Then, at some point, he would hear the music in his mind in what he described as a "round volume of sound." Pearce tells us that, "A whole concerto, symphony, quartet, or sonata, complete down to every phrase, note, and nuance, flashed into his mind in its complete form, a unity of perfection. No matter its length, *this perfect whole was perceived in a single instant.*"

He Invites the World to Dinner

One of the terrific strengths of right-brain thinkers is the desire for connection with other people. They intuitively feel connected to other humans, and enjoy making contact just for the sake of contact. Jim Hayes, an American now living in Paris, loves to make connections with people from all over the world. How does he do it? He invites them to dinner. Because, as he says, "I believe in introducing people to people."

Every Sunday for the past thirty years, he has hosted a dinner for 50 to 60 people in his home, including total strangers. In his talk on NPR's "This I Believe," he explained that anyone who calls can come, up to the seating capacity of the former sculpture studio in his home. Every Sunday a different friend prepares a feast. As he tells it, "People from all corners of the world come to break bread together, to meet, to talk, connect, and often become friends. All ages, nationalities, races, professions gather here, and since there is no organized seating, the opportunity for mingling couldn't be better." Then,

as a true right-brain thinker, he says, "I love the randomness."

"Recently, a dinner featured a typical mix: a Dutch political

cartoonist, a beautiful painter from Norway, a truck driver from

Arizona, a bookseller from Atlanta, a newspaper editor from

Sydney, students from all over, and traveling retirees."

"If I had it my way, I would introduce everyone in the whole

world to each other." To sum it up, he says, "I believe we

should know each other. After all, our lives are all connected."

FOOTBALL SUPERSTARS TOM BRADY AND ELI MANNING

Tom Brady, quarterback of the New England Patriots, is widely considered one of the best quarterbacks in the history of football. He has played in four Super Bowls, winning three of them, and twice been named the Super Bowl MVP. He led the Patriots to 21 straight wins, the longest consecutive winning streak over two seasons in the NFL.

What's his style? Sportscasters say *he has such a photographic memory, he can see every play in the playbook in his mind's eye while he is on the field.* He knows in advance where every player should be for every play. Brady has been known to look to the left to fake the defense, and then pass it to the right, where he has "seen" a receiver in his mind. This is a great example of the amazing possibilities of a right brain at work!

Another key to Brady's right-brain learning style is his take on comparing himself to others. In his "Pro Tips from Tom Brady," video, he says, "I've learned along the way not to compare yourself to any other guys. You won't be able to jump as high as some people, Vince Carter, and run as fast as Michael Vick. But I can be the best athlete I can be, and I can maximize my potential." Notice he avoids thinking there is only one "right way" to do things, and instead looks at his own potential.

Eli Manning, quarterback of the New York Giants, led his team to the 2007 Super Bowl win over the heavily-favored New England Patriots by a score of 17–14. His style is different from Tom Brady's. Sportscasters have described Manning of wanting "to do everything right," while his coaches encourage him to loosen up and enjoy the game. What's his style? The perfectionism, and striving to do everything the right way, is one of the hallmarks of left-brain thinking.

Two different styles, and two great players.

Research Intuitive - Style

Many right-brain, or intuitive, learners describe the experience of having the book they need at that moment "jump out" at them in a library or bookstore. One intuitive writer who had this happen more than once, decided to consciously rely on this amazing technique of finding just what he needed. Once he encountered a problem in his writing, or simply felt stuck, he would set his intent to find what he needed, and head off to the library. Joseph Chilton Pearce describes what happened next. "...I would simply stand and wait. When a certain detachment took the place of my ordinary, chaotic internal chatter, a pull would come, which was as powerful and as sure as though I were moved by invisible cables, and draw me to a particular section of the library. I would find myself reaching to some obscure shelf for some equally obscure book that would literally fall into my hands. I would automatically turn to the page that contained precisely what I needed to know at that time...."

Have some fun with this approach, and see if it can help you. Remember, get clear on what you need, and set your intent to have it show up for you in the library or bookstore. Go to the place you have chosen. Try the Relaxation Breathing to focus and calm down inside. Then, when you feel inclined to go in a certain direction, go ahead. Look at the books and see if one stands out for you. Some people say the books seem to have a certain shimmer around them, or maybe they are drawn to the color or the title. No matter. Pick it up and see if it is what you need. Feel free to be amazed at the results.

WHAT A WEEKEND! THE NOBEL PRIZE WORK THAT FELL INTO HIS HEAD

Gordon Gould's story is another amazing example of an enormous insight that "fell into his head," without his ever asking for it. He was a physicist who specialized in studying light. Joseph Pearce tells us that Gould "was at home for the weekend, doing nothing in particular." Then suddenly, without warning, he had a vision of enormous complexity and detail, "...etching itself into his brain indelibly in a single flash of insight.

"He reported being 'stunned, electrified,' at the enormity of it, and spent the rest of the weekend feverishly writing—page after page—the essence and remarkable implications of what he had seen. By Monday, he had roughed out the theory of laser light, for which he would eventually receive the Nobel prize.

At the time, laser light was unheard of. "Gould was mystified over such a monumental possibility falling into his head unbidden. On reflection, however, he noted that he had spent many years studying physics, and optics and had for twenty years been vigorously practicing that profession. Thus, he mused, he had been unknowingly 'feeding into the hopper of mind all the material, the bricks and mortar' for the awesome edifice that simply materialized and presented itself to him."

If you obey all the rules,
you miss all the fun.

Katharine Hepburn

THE BRAIN SURGEON WITH A MOVIE IN HIS HEAD

Allan Hamilton is a brain surgeon with an unusual talent. He graduated from Harvard Medical School, and became the Chief of Neurosurgery at the University of Arizona Health Sciences Center. He is also a script consultant for *Grey's Anatomy*. He now serves as the Executive Director of a think tank he founded to improve the practice of surgery, reducing the number of errors that take place in the operating room. We know he had to excel in a long series of rigorous studies over many years to achieve his prestigious professional position. He has obviously put his left-brain to good use! And, isn't that what we would want from someone who was going to operate on our brain?

But, in his own words, Dr. Hamilton says he has had to unlearn some of his formal education in order to access even better ways to operate. In his book, *The Scalpel and the Soul*, he describes his unusual preparation for surgery.

Before any big operation, he has a ritual of taking a long shower and visualizing the whole surgery in his mind's eye. "The operation seems to roll like a movie behind my closed eyes as I stand in the shower," he explains. He describes checking to make sure all the instruments are in place, and that the power panel and all of the electrical equipment are working properly. Then, amazingly, he watches as he performs the surgery from beginning to end. In an experience of time that is probably familiar to you by now, he notes: "Everything feels like it's happening at the same speed it would if I were actually in the operating room. But usually, when I look at the clock next to the shower, I've visualized the entire procedure in five minutes, no matter who long, or how complex the operation.

"I've discovered that the 'inner eye' in my right brain can see potential problems that my analytic left brain can't identify. I envision the entire surgical procedure with the end result clearly in mind. I've rarely had an instance where the mental visualization led me astray. In the beginning, I had a hard time listening to my inner voice and trusting it, letting it guide me. But this visualization process has always worked. I get a pre-existing image of the surgery. I tap into it and it teaches me."

IN THE BLINK OF AN EYE

In his number one bestseller *Blink,* author Malcolm Gladwell focuses on people's ability to make snap judgments based on their instincts, gut reactions, and other mysterious processes. Consider one of his stories to see if you may have had similar experiences in your own life. I'm betting you have.

Gladwell tells the story of a potentially rare and valuable art find. In 1983, an art dealer named Gianfranco Becchina approached the famous J. Paul Getty museum in California. The dealer claimed to have a rare marble statue dating back to the sixth century BC. There are less than two hundred of this type of statue, known as a kouros, in the world, and most are damaged or in fragments. His statue was in almost perfect condition. His asking price was $10 million.

The Getty museum was cautious, and took over fourteen months to study the statue in great detail to verify its authenticity. They brought in their team of lawyers to exam the historical records verifying the age and ownership of the art, and they pronounced them sound. A geologist was hired, who examined it with an array of sophisticated instruments. Armed with an electron microscope, a mass spectrometer, and a variety of x-rays, he determined the statue to be thousands of years old, and not a recent fake. Based on all of this evidence, the Getty decided to purchase the statue. To great fanfare, they put it on display. Only then did they begin to hear from the art historians who instinctively knew something was amiss.

Although they couldn't articulate their reasons, all said essentially the same thing: If you haven't paid for it yet, don't! And if you have, try and get your money back. As one prestigious museum director explained, when he looked at the statue, he felt "a wave of 'intuitive repulsion.'" Several other art historians agreed, based largely on their feelings and gut reactions. They said it just didn't look right.

The museum had a problem. They had to find out who was right. Was it their lawyers and scientists, who had studied it for over a year? Or was it a group of art historians who took one glance and immediately dismissed it as a fraud? Were they to believe fourteen months of study, or two seconds of intuitive response?

As it turns out, the art directors with their intuitive response got it right. The statue was a fake that had been made in Rome in the early 1980s. The conclusion will sound very familiar to any student who can "read" a situation, or who just knows she knows an answer, without being able to explain it. As Gladwell says, "In the first two seconds of looking—in a single glance—they were able to understand more about the essence of the statue than the team at the Getty was able to understand after fourteen months."